THE MEDITERRANEAN DIET COOKBOOK FOR TWO

Effortless Recipes Perfectly Portioned for Pairs

HEALTHY & DELICIOUS MEALS FOR EVERY DAY

Kathrin Narrell

DISCLAIMER

The recipes and information in this book are provided for educational purposes only. Please always consult a licensed professional before making changes to your lifestyle or diet. The author and publisher shall have neither liability nor responsibility to anyone with respect to any loss or damage caused or alleged to be caused directly or indirectly by the information contained in this book. All trademarks and brands within this book are for clarifying purposes only and are owned by the owners themselves, not affiliated with this document.

Images from shutterstock.com

CONTENTS

CONCLUSION

INTRODUCTION

The Mediterranean diet incorporates the traditional healthy lifestyles of people from countries including France, Greece, Italy, and Spain. It's generally accepted that these people live longer and suffer less from cancer and cardiovascular disease than most Americans do, so there's a lot we can learn from them, as there are benefits we can get. Especially when multiplied for two persons.

This is the perfect cookbook to create efficiency in the kitchen and grocery store while still producing nutritious, interesting meals for healthy eating and weight loss.

Two-serving cooking is one of the biggest challenges when trying to adhere to a healthy eating plan. All recipes are portioned for 2 servings, which means you won't be eating the same thing for a week or trying to adjust recipes and struggling to figure out proper cooking times and fractions of measurements.

This is your starting point to living happier and healthier by embracing the Mediterranean diet.

RIZOGALO

SERVINGS: 2 PREP TIME: 5 min. COOK TIME: 45 min.

CARBS – 25 g FAT – 11 g PROTEIN – 8 g CALORIES – 234

INGREDIENTS

- *1 Tbsp butter*
- *½ quart milk*
- *1 pinch of salt*
- *¼ cup rice*
- *3" strip of lemon rind*
- *⅛ cup sugar*
- *1 egg (beaten well)*
- *½ tsp vanilla extract*
- *1 dash ground cinnamon*

DIRECTIONS

1. Melt butter over medium-high in a large saucepan.
2. Add milk and salt. Bring it to a boil.
3. Add lemon rind and rice, boil for 25 minutes or more, stirring to avoid sticking to the bottom. Rice should be tender but not mushy.
4. Discard lemon rind and stir in sugar.
5. Beat eggs in a bowl, then add 1 cup warm mixture from the saucepan to temper and prevent eggs from curdling.
6. Reduce to low and pour egg mixture into the pot, stirring all the time, and cook until it begins to thicken.
7. Stir in vanilla and remove from heat. Let it cool.
8. Dust with cinnamon before serving.

PROVENCE BAKED EGGS

SERVINGS: 2 PREP TIME: 15 min. COOK TIME: 15 min.

CARBS – 5 g FAT – 33 g PROTEIN – 60 g CALORIES – 575

INGREDIENTS

1 tsp Herbes de Provence
6 eggs
4 slices smoked turkey
½ cup cheddar cheese, cubed
½ cup milk or cream
2 tsp parmesan cheese
½ tsp paprika
2 Tbsp butter or oil
salt and pepper, to taste

DIRECTIONS

1. Preheat oven to 390°F, set the oven rack on the middle level.
2. Butter two oven safe serving dish.
3. Add cheddar and the slices cold cut meat
4. Whisk milk, Herbes de Provence, cheese, salt, paprika, and pepper.
5. Drizzle 1 Tbsp of milk herb mix on the pan.
6. Bake eggs for 15-20 minutes or until you get desired doneness.

QUARK AND CUCUMBER TOASTS

SERVINGS: 2 PREP TIME: 5 min. COOK TIME: 5 min.

CARBS – 13 g FAT – 5 g PROTEIN – 7 g CALORIES – 141

INGREDIENTS

- *2 slices whole-grain bread, toasted*
- *2 Tbsp quark*
- *2 Tbsp shaved cucumber*
- *1 Tbsp dill*
- *1 pinch sea salt*

DIRECTIONS

1. Top each toast with quark, cucumber, dill, and sea salt.

TIGANOPSOMO

SERVINGS: 2 PREP TIME: 10 min. COOK TIME: 35 min.

CARBS – 44 g FAT – 7 g PROTEIN – 8 g CALORIES – 269

INGREDIENTS

250 grams flour
3,5 grams dried yeast
150 grams lukewarm water
¼ tsp sugar
¼ tsp salt
1½ Tbsp chopped rosemary, mint, parsley, sage, oregano
1 Tbsp olive oil
100 grams feta cheese
Extra olive oil for frying
balsamic vinegar to drizzle on top

DIRECTIONS

1. Mix all components until you get a soft dough. Leave it to rest for 30 minutes.
2. Divide dough evenly into 4 balls and flatten each one using a roller.
3. Add to each piece a part of cheese and herbs.
4. Fold dough around filling and flatten it again.
5. Preheat olive oil in a frying pan on low heat.
6. Bake for 15-20 minutes or so, turning them often until bread turns golden brown.
7. Serve bread on a plate with some balsamic vinegar. Makes two portions of two tiganopsomo breads.

FIG AND RICOTTA OATS

SERVINGS: 2 PREP TIME: 8 h. COOK TIME: 10 min.

CARBS – 47 g FAT – 8 g PROTEIN – 10 g CALORIES – 294

INGREDIENTS

- *1 cup old-fashioned rolled oats*
- *1 cup water*
- *2 Pinches of salt*
- *4 Tbsp part-skim ricotta cheese*
- *4 Tbsp chopped dried figs*
- *2 Tbsp toasted sliced almonds*
- *4 tsp honey*

DIRECTIONS

1. Mix oats, water, and salt in a jar and stir. Cover with lid and put in the fridge overnight.
2. In the morning, heat oats, if desired. Top with figs, ricotta, almonds and honey.

QUICK PAELLA SOUP

SERVINGS: 2 PREP TIME: 10 min. COOK TIME: 25 min.

CARBS – 34 g FAT – 8 g PROTEIN – 10 g CALORIES – 270

INGREDIENTS

1 Tbsp canola oil
1 small onion, chopped
1 small green bell pepper, chopped
1 garlic clove, minced
1 small red bell pepper, chopped
1½ cups uncooked quick-cooking brown rice
½ (14-ounce) can fat-free, less-sodium chicken broth
½ tsp ground turmeric
¼ tsp dried thyme
½ tsp smoked paprika
½ can (14-ounce) can petite diced tomatoes
1 cup tomato juice
½ cup frozen green peas
¼ pound medium shrimp, peeled and deveined
Freshly ground black pepper, to taste

DIRECTIONS

1. In a large stockpot over medium heat, heat oil.
2. Add onions, bell peppers and garlic. Sauté for 6 minutes.
3. Stir in rice, broth, ¾ cups water, turmeric, thyme, and smoked paprika. Bring to a boil. Cover, reduce heat to medium-low, and cook for 10 minutes.
4. Stir in remaining ingredients and cook 4-5 minutes, until shrimp is pink and tender.

ROASTED CARROT SOUP WITH GINGER

SERVINGS: 2 PREP TIME: 15 min. COOK TIME: 1 h. 15 min.

CARBS – 15 g FAT – 8 g PROTEIN – 4 g CALORIES – 140

INGREDIENTS

- ½ Tbsp olive oil
- ½ pound carrots, peeled and cut into 3" lengths
- ½ small onion, cut into medium dices
- ½ Tbsp unsalted butter
- ½ Tbsp fresh minced ginger
- 1 small rib celery, cut into medium dices
- ½ tsp kosher salt
- 1 cup homemade or low-salt chicken broth
- Chopped fresh chervil or chives, for garnish
- ⅛ tsp ground white pepper

DIRECTIONS

1. Heat the oven to 375°F.
2. In a medium baking dish, place the carrots and drizzle with the olive oil. Toss to coat well.
3. Roast in the oven, stirring once halfway through, until they're blistered and tender, about 1 hour.
4. In a medium heavy saucepan over medium heat, melt the butter.
5. Add the onion and cook 2-3 minutes.
6. Stir in the ginger and celery. Cook until the onions start to brown and the celery softens a bit, 4-5 minutes.
7. Add the chicken broth, carrots, 1 cup of water, pepper, and salt. Bring to a boil, lower the heat to medium-low, and cover. Cook at a lively simmer for about 45 minutes.
8. Switch off the heat and allow the soup to cool.
9. Purée the soup in a blender in batches, never filling the blender more than a third full.
10. Before serving, transfer the soup to the po and reheat.
11. Garnish with the chervil or chives.

PROVENCAL-STYLE GARLIC SOUP

SERVINGS: 2 PREP TIME: 15 min. COOK TIME: 20 min.

CARBS – 13 g FAT – 6 g PROTEIN – 3 g CALORIES – 120

INGREDIENTS

6 cloves garlic, halved
1 Tbsp olive oil
3 cups chicken broth
½ tsp dried sage
1 pinch of saffron
2 slices country bread, toasted
100 g Gruyère cheese, grated
2 fried eggs
salt and pepper, to taste

DIRECTIONS

1. Soften garlic in oil in a saucepan. Add in broth and sage. Cover and simmer for 15 minutes.
2. Remove sage and garlic. Season to taste with salt and pepper.
3. In a bowl, crush garlic using a back of spoon. Back garlic in the broth and add saffron.
4. Sprinkle the top of bread slices with cheese and top with fried egg. Serve with soup.

AVGOLEMONO LEMON CHICKEN SOUP

SERVINGS: 2 PREP TIME: 30 min. COOK TIME: 35 min.

CARBS – 33 g FAT – 7 g PROTEIN – 17 g CALORIES – 236

INGREDIENTS

- *1-2 Tbsp extra-virgin olive oil*
- *½ cup carrots, finely chopped*
- *½ cup celery, finely chopped*
- *½ cup green onions, finely chopped*
- *1 garlic clove, finely chopped*
- *3 cups low-sodium chicken broth*
- *1 bay leaves*
- *½ cup rice*
- *salt and pepper, to taste*
- *1 cooked boneless chicken breast pieces, shredded*
- *¼ cup freshly-squeezed lemon juice*
- *1 large eggs*

DIRECTIONS

1. On medium-high, heat 1 Tbsp olive oil in a heavy pot.
2. Add carrots, celery and green onions, stir to cook briefly, then add in garlic.
3. Add broth and bay leaves, turn to high heat. Once it started to a boil, add rice, salt, and pepper to taste.
4. Turn to medium-low and simmer for 20 minutes or until the rice is tender. Now sti in the cooked chicken.
5. Add eggs and lemon juice in a bowl and whisk well. Add 2 ladles of broth from the pot while whisking. Once combined, add sauce to the soup and stir. Remove from heat.
6. Garnish with fresh parsley, if desired.

LIME SHRIMP AND AVOCADO SALAD

SERVINGS: 2 PREP TIME: 5 min. COOK TIME: 15 min.

CARBS – 15 g FAT – 8 g PROTEIN – 4 g CALORIES – 140

INGREDIENTS

¼ cup red onion, chopped
2 limes juice
1 tsp olive oil
¼ tsp salt, black pepper to taste
1 lb. jumbo cooked, peeled shrimp
1 tomato, diced
1 hass avocado, diced
1 jalapeno, seeds removed, diced fine
1 Tbsp chopped cilantro

DIRECTIONS

1. Mix onion, lime juice, oil, salt, and pepper in a small bowl. Marinate for 15 minutes.
2. Mix shrimp, avocado, tomato, jalapeño in a large bowl.
3. Mix all ingredients, add cilantro, and toss.

ITALIAN SANDWICHES WITH OLIVE TAPENADE

SERVINGS: 2 PREP TIME: 5 min. COOK TIME: 5 min.

CARBS – 6 g FAT – 20 g PROTEIN – 33 g CALORIES – 392

INGREDIENTS

- *2 rolls ciabatta bread*
- *⅓ lb. salami thin sliced*
- *4 slices provolone cheese*
- *¼ cup kalamata olives pitted, chopped*
- *⅛ cup balsamic vinegar*
- *½ cup arugula lettuce (optional)*

DIRECTIONS

1. Mix olives with vinegar to make tapenade.
2. Spread on the bread and top with lettuce (if used), cheese, and salami.

PINEAPPLE AND ARUGULA SALAD

SERVINGS: 2 PREP TIME: 10 min. COOK TIME: 5 min.

CARBS – 8 g FAT – 4 g PROTEIN – 1 g CALORIES – 64

INGREDIENTS

2 cups torn arugula leaves
⅛ fresh pineapple, cut into 1-in slices
⅛ red onion, thinly sliced
⅛ cup fresh cilantro, chopped
1½ Tbsp apple cider vinegar
½ Tbsp olive oil
1 tsp maple syrup (or honey)
⅛ tsp salt

DIRECTIONS

1. Place the pineapple slices on a hot grill and grill on both sides until the fruit is slightly caramelized and grill marks appear. Remove the pineapple and let cool.
2. When pineapple has cooled, cut into chunks.
3. Mix pineapple, arugula, cilantro, and red onion in a salad bowl.
4. Whisk together the olive oil, apple cider vinegar, salt and maple syrup in a small bowl. Pour this dressing over the salad and toss to coat.

HALIBUT SANDWICHES

SERVINGS: 2 PREP TIME: 20 min. COOK TIME: 20 min.

CARBS – 51 g FAT – 12 g PROTEIN – 24 g CALORIES – 419

INGREDIENTS

- *2 (6-ounce) halibut fillets, skin removed*
- *Kosher salt and freshly ground black pepper, to taste*
- *2 Tbsps + 1 tsp olive oil, divided*
- *1 garlic clove, halved*
- *1 (14-ounce) loaf ciabatta bread, ends trimmed, split in half horizontally, sliced*
- *¼ cup sun-dried tomatoes, chopped*
- *¼ cup reduced-fat mayonnaise*
- *2 Tbsps fresh flat-leaf parsley, chopped*
- *¼ cup chopped fresh basil*
- *Zest of 1 large lemon*
- *1 Tbsp capers, drained and mashed*
- *2 packed cups arugula*

DIRECTIONS

1. Preheat oven to 450°F.
2. Spray a small baking dish cooking spray.
3. Place halibut in dish and season with a tsp of olive oil. Bake 10-15 minutes, until the flesh flakes easily with a fork and cooked through. Cool.
4. Brush bread slices with two Tbsps olive oil Bake on a baking sheet until golden, about 6-8 minutes.
5. Rub toasted surfaces with garlic.
6. Combine sun-dried tomatoes, mayonnaise basil, parsley, capers, and lemon zest in a medium bowl.
7. Add fish, mixing and flaking with a fork.
8. Spoon onto the bottom half of bread and place arugula on the top. Add top of bread

MEDITERRANEAN GRILLED EGGPLANT

SERVINGS: 2 PREP TIME: 15 min. COOK TIME: 45 min.

CARBS – 11 g FAT – 13 g PROTEIN – 1 g CALORIES – 163

INGREDIENTS

FOR EGGPLANT
½ cup extra-virgin olive oil
1 tsp dried oregano
¼ tsp crushed red pepper flakes
kosher salt and black pepper, to taste
2 eggplants, sliced into ¼" rounds
¼ cup crumbled feta
1 Tbsp freshly chopped parsley
¼ lemon juice

FOR TAHINI
⅓ cup tahini
1 lemon juice

- 2 Tbsp water
- 1 clove garlic, minced
- kosher salt, to taste

DIRECTIONS

1. Preheat grill and grill eggplant slices for 7 minutes per or so until soften and have grill marks.
2. Top grilled eggplants with feta and parsley, then squeeze lemon juice over.
3. To make dressing, whisk tahini, lemon juice, water, and garlic in a medium bowl. Season with salt.
4. Serve warm with tahini dressing.

MELITZANOSALATA

CARBS – 3 g FAT – 9 g PROTEIN – 1 g CALORIES – 122

INGREDIENTS

- *2 large eggplants*
- *4 cloves garlic, peeled and minced*
- *¼ cup extra-virgin olive oil*
- *3 Tbsp lemon juice*
- *¾ tsp kosher salt*
- *¼ tsp pepper*
- *fresh dill and olives, for garnish*

DIRECTIONS

1. Preheat oven to 400°F.
2. Arrange eggplants on a baking sheet, lined with foil, and prick with a fork. Roast for 1 hour, turning every 15 minutes, until charred and soft. Remove from oven and le them cool.
3. Peel eggplants and chop. Transfer in a colander for 15 minutes.
4. Move drained eggplant to a large bowl and mash with a fork.
5. Add garlic, olive oil, lemon juice, salt, and pepper.
6. Chill for one hour. Garnish with dill and olives.

MEDITERRANEAN THIN-CRUST FLABREAD

SERVINGS: 2 PREP TIME: 15 min. COOK TIME: 1 h. 15 min.

CARBS – 15 g FAT – 8 g PROTEIN – 4 g CALORIES – 140

INGREDIENTS

FOR DOUGH:
¾ cup lukewarm water
1 tsp instant yeast
2 cup all-purpose flour
1½ tsp salt

FOR TOPPINGS:
1 garlic clove, crushed
1 Tbsp olive oil
¼ tsp sea salt (plus a pinch)
½ tomato, thinly sliced
¼ yellow beet, thinly sliced
½ meyer lemon, thinly sliced
¼ potato, thinly sliced
1 radish, thinly sliced
½ burrata mozarella ball, dotted all over the flatbread
1 heaping Tbsp fresh tarragon, finely chopped

DIRECTIONS

1. Mix the water and the yeast in a mixing bowl, stir to dissolve the yeast. Add the flour and salt, and mix until the shaggy dough is formed.
2. Turn the dough out to a clean place to work. Knead until all the flour is mixed in and the dough is smooth and elastic for about 5 minutes.
3. Cover the dough with a mixing bowl or a clean kitchen towel while preparing the toppings.
4. Preheat the oven to 375 F.
5. Roll out the flatbread. Brush the olive oil all over, even on the edges.
6. Rub the crushed garlic throughout the dough, allowing the pieces to be broken off at random. Sprinkle with salt (keep the pinch for later).
7. Lay the toppings, completely covering the dough. Scatter the cheese all over. Sprinkle with salt.
8. Bake for 20-25 minutes or until vegetables look fairly crisped and the edges of pizza have browned!

CREOLE SPAGHETTI

CARBS – 57 g FAT – 8 g PROTEIN – 4 g CALORIES – 413

INGREDIENTS

- *1 extra virgin olive oil*
- *1¼ lbs. ground beef (85% lean)*
- *¼ lb country ham, cut into ¼" pieces (about ¾ cup)*
- *1 can tomato sauce*
- *½ cup sofrito*
- *½ Tbsp minced garlic*
- *½ Tbsp sugar*
- *¼ tsp ground cumin*
- *¼ tsp oregano*
- *¼ packet sazon with coriander & annatto*
- *¼ cup manzanillo olives stuffed with minced pimientos, chopped*
- *½ cup finely chopped fresh cilantro, divided*
- *½ tsp. adobo all-purpose seasoning with pepper*
- *½ lb. spaghetti*
- *parmesan cheese, to taste*

DIRECTIONS

1. Over medium-high, heat olive oil in a skillet and add beef. Cook until browned, about 6 minutes.
2. Transfer the beef over to the plate.
3. Reheat the pan over medium heat and add the ham. Cook, stirring occasionally, for about 4 minutes, until the ham is golden brown.
4. Add tomato sauce, garlic, sugar, cumin, oregano and sazon to the pan. Cook until the mixture of tomato sauce starts to bubble.
5. Stir in reserved beef, olives, 1/8 cup coriander and Adobo. Simmer, stirring occasionally, until sauce thickens and flavors, about 8 minutes longer. Stir in the remaining coriander.
6. Cook spaghetti according to the manufacture's instructions.
7. Strain pasta, reserve 1½ cups water.
8. Add reserved pasta water and spaghetti to skillet with sauce over medium-high heat.
9. Toss spaghetti with sauce for 3 minutes, using tongs.
10. Serve with Parmesan cheese.

MEDITERRANEAN PIAZZA WITH FETA CHEESE

SERVINGS: 2 PREP TIME: 10 min. COOK TIME: 30 min.

CARBS – 124 g FAT – 21 g PROTEIN – 24 g CALORIES – 779

INGREDIENTS

1 pound pizza dough
cornmeal for dusting the pizza peel
¼ cup pizza sauce
2-3 large roasted red peppers from a can, chopped
¼ cup pitted Kalamata olives
¼ cup crumbled feta cheese
2 Tbsp chopped green onions

DIRECTIONS

1. Preheat oven to 450°F.
2. Use a pizza stone, if you have it and set it in the oven.
3. On a baking sheet, sprinkle cornmeal.
4. Divide dough in two pieces, form circles from each one. Stretch the dough, where necessary.
5. Divide sauce between pizzas, spread it on top, leaving 1" around edges. Add olives.
6. Bake for 7-8 minutes, then add feta cheese and bake for 2 more minutes. Edges should be golden, feta should be just warmed up at the end.
7. Remove from oven, let it sit for 2-3 minutes at room temperature).

PACCHERI AL FORNO

SERVINGS: 2 PREP TIME: 10 min. COOK TIME: 30 min.

CARBS – 21 g FAT – 8 g PROTEIN – 6 g CALORIES – 160

INGREDIENTS

- ½ bag paccheri
- 1 can cherry tomatoes
- ½ pound mozzarella, cut into ½" cubes
- ¼ cup flat-leaf parsley, finely chopped
- ½ cup cow's milk ricotta
- extra-virgin olive oil, to taste
- 1½ ounces Parmigiano Reggiano, grated
- 1 garlic clove, finely chopped
- sea salt and pepper, to taste

DIRECTIONS

1. Preheat the oven to 400°F.
2. Bring a pot of cold water to a boil, then season with salt.
3. Mix olive oil with garlic in a large skillet. Cook over medium-high heat until oil starts to bubble.
4. Add tomatoes and salt. Cook, occasionally stirring, for 3 minutes.
5. Cover it and remove pan from heat.
6. Combine mozzarella, ricotta and parsley in a medium bowl.
7. Drop the pasta in the pot when the water boils and cook, stirring frequently, until the pasta is very al dente.
8. Drain the pasta and place in a 9"-by-13" ovenproof gratin or baking dish. When slightly chilled, add half of the cheese mixture to the pasta, add tomato sauce to the top and finish with the rest cheese.
9. Bake for 25 minutes, or until mozzarella has melted and the golden crust is formed
10. Take out from oven and sprinkle it with Parmigiano.
11. Allow to melt for 5 minutes and serve with the rest grated cheese.

FIDEUA PASTA PAELLA

SERVINGS: 2 PREP TIME: 5 min. COOK TIME: 45 min.

CARBS – 78 g FAT – 25 g PROTEIN – 66 g CALORIES – 817

INGREDIENTS

- ½ bronzini whole
- ¼ lb shrimp/prawns 225g, shell on
- ½ stick celery
- ½ carrot small, cleaned but no need to peel or take ends off
- 1 stems parsley
- ½ sprig thyme
- 2½ Tbsp olive oil approx
- ½ Spanish onion
- ½ red pepper
- ¼ tsp paprika
- 1½ cloves garlic
- ¼ tsp fennel seeds
- 7 oz crushed tomatoes 400g, 1 can
- 1 small pinches around 15 threads saffron
- 6 oz pasta 340g, fideos/broken spaghetti
- ¼ lb clams 225g

DIRECTIONS

Remove the shells from shrimps, but keep them.

Make stock by putting the fish bones, the shrimp shells, the celery, the carrot, the parsley stems, the sprig of thyme and the small wedge of the onion in a pot and cover with water. You'll need to add about 4 cups of water to the pot. Then bring to a boil and reduce to a simmer (covered).

3. In the meantime, chop the remaining onion, pepper, and garlic.
4. Heat 2 Tbsps of olive oil in a large skillet over medium-low heat and fry the fish and shrimp gently until they are almost cooked through. Remove and set aside from the pan.
5. Add the remaining oil, then add the onion and the pepper to the skillet.
6. Cook for about 10 minutes, stirring. Add the paprika, garlic and fennel seeds.
7. Now the stock should be ready; strain it to remove all the bones and vegetables.
8. Cook the onions and the mixture of spices for another 5 minutes, then add the tomatoes. Cook a few minutes, then add the pasta.
9. Stir well so that the oily mixture is covered and cook for a few more minutes.
10. Add stock to the pan and stir. Leave to cook in a simmer for 10 minutes.
11. Stir, then add the clams and place them under the liquid and the pasta. Cook for a minute, add shrimp and fish.
12. After about 5 minutes, the clams should open and everything should be ready.

SHRIMP PASTA WITH ROSEMARY SAUSE

SERVINGS: 2 PREP TIME: 10 min. COOK TIME: 20 min.

CARBS – 14 g FAT – 5 g PROTEIN – 8 g CALORIES – 225

INGREDIENTS

- *2 Tbsp butter*
- *½ Tbsp fresh thyme*
- *½ Tbsp fresh rosemary*
- *5 ounces shrimp, peeled, deveined*
- *1½ Tbsp flour*
- *12 ounces milk, warm*
- *¼ onion, chopped*
- *½ cup fresh parsley*
- *¼ cup green onion, or chives*
- *Salt and pepper, to taste*
- *½ tsp nutmeg*
- *Juie of ¼ lime*
- *5 ounces pasta, cooked*

DIRECTIONS

1. Add butter, rosemary, and thyme to a large pan. Stir.
2. Add the shrimp and cook for 3 minutes.
3. Remove from pan and set aside.
4. Sprinkle the flour into the rosemary sauce and mix until it becomes slightly brown.
5. Continue stirring and add the warm milk slowly.
6. Add salt, ground nutmeg, and pepper.
7. Stir and add the chopped onion. Cook for 5 minutes.
8. Add the green onion and fresh parsley. Remove the pan from the stove. Blend everything with a hand blender in the pan.
9. Cook until the sauce is bubbling, then turn off the heat.
10. Add the shrimp and stir to coat in sauce.
11. Add the lime juice.
12. Stir in the pasta.
13. Sprinkle with chopped parsley and serve.

MEDITERRANEAN BAKED DIJON SALMON

SERVINGS: 2 PREP TIME: 5 min. COOK TIME: 20 min.

CARBS – 10 g FAT – 23 g PROTEIN – 48 g CALORIES – 441

INGREDIENTS

1 lb. salmon fillet
⅓ cup Dijon mustard
1 Tbsp olive oil
2 Tbsp lemon juice
¼ tsp salt
1 Tbsp fresh dill, chopped
4 cloves garlic, minced
1 Tbsp capers

DIRECTIONS

1. Preheat oven to 400°F and, using parchment paper, line a baking sheet.
2. Place salmon on the baking sheet skin side down.
3. Mix mustard, oil, lemon juice, salt, dill, garlic and capers in a small bowl.
4. Brush salmon with mixture.
5. Bake for 18-23 minutes depending on the thickness.

GREEK SALMON

CARBS – 6 g FAT – 11 g PROTEIN – 14 g CALORIES – 281

INGREDIENTS

- *1 Tbsp olive oil*
- *½ medium onion, cut into medium dices*
- *½ Tbsp unsalted butter*
- *½ pound carrots, peeled and cut*
- *½ Tbsp fresh minced ginger*
- *½ large rib celery, cut into medium dices*
- *½ tsp kosher salt*
- *1 cup chicken broth*
- *Chopped fresh chervil or chives, for garnish*
- *⅛ tsp ground white pepper*

DIRECTIONS

1. Preheat oven to 375°F.
2. Whisk oil, lemon juice, garlic, oregano, pepper flakes, pepper in a large bowl, then add in feta. Cover and set feta marinade in the fridge for 10 minutes.
3. Scatter lemon slices and onion at the bottom of a baking dish.
4. Add fillets to the baking dish, skin side down. Season with salt and pepper.
5. Bake for 20 minutes or more until flaky and opaque.
6. Add tomatoes, olives, cucumbers, onion, and dill into the bowl with feta. Fold to combine.
7. Plate salmon with feta mixture on top.

LEBANESE FISH WITH HERBY TAHINI

SERVINGS: 2 PREP TIME: 15 min. COOK TIME: 1 h. 15 min.

CARBS – 88 g FAT – 13 g PROTEIN – 28 g CALORIES – 582

INGREDIENTS

FOR TAHINI AND RICE

1 cloves garlic
½ bunch flat-leaf parsley
½ cup tahini
¼ cup freshly squeezed lemon juice
½ cup water
1 pinch salt, or to taste
½ cup basmati rice
2 Tbsp clarified butter
1 Tbsp extra-virgin olive oil
½ yellow onion, peeled and sliced into ¼"
rings
¼ cup pine nuts

FOR FISH

1 pound fish filet
1 Tbsp olive oil
1 pinch salt and pepper
1 Tbsp butter
2 lime, quartered
½ bunch cilantro or parsley

DIRECTIONS

Pulse garlic and parsley in a food
processor, then add tahini.

2. Blend garlic, parsley, and tahini well. Add lemon juice and blend again.
3. Add salt and drizzle water while processing until it thins out to a pourable consistency.
4. Preheat oven to 500°F.
5. Heat olive oil in a sauté pan, and add onion with salt. Stir and cook over high heat until the onions are brown and caramelized. Drain and reserve.
6. Fry pine nuts in butter until they are golden. Drain and reserve.
7. Set a pot of water on to boil and salt. When it comes to a boil, add and cook rice for 10 minutes.
8. While rice is cooking, rub flesh of fish with oil, salt and pepper, and bake for 20-25 minutes or more until it's cooked through.
9. Drain cooked rice, toss it with 2 Tbsps of butter, onions, and pine nuts. Reserve some pine nuts and onions for garnishing.
10. Add rice on a platter and top with fish. Pour enough tahini over fish.
11. Garnish with cilantro, reserved onions and pine nuts. Serve warm or room temperature.

BAKED FISH WITH SUMAC AND OREGANO SPICES

SERVINGS: 2 PREP TIME: 20 min. COOK TIME: 30 min.

CARBS – 15 g FAT – 8 g PROTEIN – 4 g CALORIES – 140

INGREDIENTS

- *1½ lbs. fresh fish, rinsed*
- *1 bell pepper, finely chopped*
- *1 sweet red pepper, finely chopped*
- *½ garlic head, crushed*
- *2 lemons, juiced*
- *3 tsps ground thyme*
- *1 tsps ground cilantro*
- *3 tsps quality sumac*
- *5 tsps olive oil*
- *½ tsp salt, to taste*

DIRECTIONS

1. Preheat oven to 350°F.
2. Place fish on a baking tray and rub with a salt and 1 tsps thyme, place a few lemon slices inside and bake for 20 minutes.
3. Mix garlic, peppers, lemon juice, 2 tsps thyme, cilantro, sumac, oil and salt to taste.
4. Once fish is baked, let it cool a little, then remove bones and scales, then back it in a tray and top with the paste.
5. Bake for 10 minutes more so the paste infuses into the fish.

SPICY SHRIMP IN A POT

SERVINGS: 2 PREP TIME: 30 min. COOK TIME: 30 min.

CARBS – 8 g FAT – 6 g PROTEIN – 10 g CALORIES – 119

INGREDIENTS

½ pound shrimp
1 or 2 cloves garlic, diced
1 small onion, diced
1½ Tbsp olive oil
2 ripe tomatoes, peeled and diced
2 Hungarian wax peppers or 1 green Bell pepper
3 tsp tomato paste
½ cup small button mushrooms
½ tsp salt
⅛ tsp black pepper
⅛ tsp hot red pepper flakes
½ cup grated mild yellow cheese

DIRECTIONS

Boil shrimp in salted boiling water for 1 to 2 minutes. Drain them and run under cold water.

2. Heat olive oil in a saucepan and fry the garlic and onions until they soften and semitransparent.
3. Add the green peppers and cook 3 minutes more.
4. Add the diced tomatoes, mushrooms, spices and tomato paste, and allow the mixture to simmer until most of the liquid is gone.
5. Add the shrimps and gently stir with a wooden spoon.
6. Place the mixture into one large or several small clay pots. Generously cover the top(s) with grated cheese.
7. Put the casserole(s) in the oven set on the broil setting on a rack near the top. Cook until the cheese browns nicely and bubbly. Remove the casserole and serve immediately while it's hot.

SHISH KEBABS

SERVINGS: 2 PREP TIME: 8 h. COOK TIME: 10 min.

CARBS – 38 g FAT – 5 g PROTEIN – 27 g CALORIES – 306

INGREDIENTS

- ½ cup sugar
- ½ cup reduced-sodium soy sauce
- ½ cup ketchup
- 1 tsp garlic powder
- 1 tsp ground ginger
- 1 pounds sirloin steak, cut into 1½" cubes
- 1-2 small zucchini, cut into 1" slices
- ¼ pound medium fresh mushrooms
- 1 sweet red/green pepper, cut into 1" pieces
- 4-5 cherry tomatoes, halved
- 1 small onion, cut into 1" pieces
- 1 cup cubed fresh pineapple

DIRECTIONS

1. Mix first five ingredients for the marinade.
2. Place half of the marinade and beef in a large plastic bag; turn to coat and seal the bag, allowing to marinate overnight.
3. Reserve and cover the remaining marinade
4. Thread beef, vegetables, and pineapple on metal or wooden skewers.
5. Grill, covered, over medium heat until beef reaches desired doneness and vegetables are tender, occasionally turning, 12-15 minutes.
6. Boil the reserved marinade in a small saucepan, stirring occasionally, about 1 minute. Serve with kebabs.

GRILLED STEAK WITH BARLEY SALAD

SERVINGS: 2 PREP TIME: 25 min. COOK TIME: 15 min.

CARBS – 48 g FAT – 23 g PROTEIN – 28 g CALORIES – 508

INGREDIENTS

1 tsp Italian seasoning blend
½ pound flank steak, trimmed
⅛ tsp black pepper
¼ tsp salt
1 cup cooked barley
½ (15 oz) can no salt added chickpeas, drained and rinsed
¼ cup chopped roasted tomatoes
1 cucumber, seeded and diced
⅛ cup chopped fresh basil
¼ cup lemon juice
⅛ cup crumbled feta
⅛ cup pitted Kalamata olives, chopped

DIRECTIONS

1. Heat a grill pan over medium-high or heat a grill to medium-high.
2. Dry steak with a paper towel and sprinkle both sides with Italian seasoning, pepper and ¼ tsp salt.
3. Grill steak 4-6 minutes for each side or until it reaches desired degree of doneness.
4. Transfer to a foiled cutting board and allow to rest 5 minutes, then cut into thin strips across the grain.
5. In a medium bowl, combine remaining ingredients.

LAMB QUINOA BURGERS

SERVINGS: 2 PREP TIME: 10 min. COOK TIME: 15 min.

CARBS – 19 g FAT – 40 g PROTEIN – 21 g CALORIES – 526

INGREDIENTS

FOR LAMB BURGERS:
- ¼ cup Della Basmati & Quinoa mixture, cooked
- ½ pound ground lamb
- ⅛ tsp salt
- ¼ tsp paprika
- ⅛ tsp garlic powder
- ⅛ tsp onion powder
- ¼ tsp rosemary
- ⅛ tsp cayenne red pepper
- ⅛ cup olive oil

FOR OPTIONAL MINT-YOGURT SAUCE:
- ¼ cup plain yogurt
- 3 tsp fresh, chopped mint

DIRECTIONS

1. Mix together all ingredients until combined.
2. Make four lamb burger patties from the mixture.
3. Prepare your grill to medium-low heat.
4. Cook the burgers, flipping once, until golden-brown and cooked your liking.
5. While the burgers are cooking, combine the chopped mint and yogurt in a small bowl and stir until combined.
6. Serve on a hamburger bun with a dollop of mint-yogurt. Garnish with greens, tomato, and onion if desired.

CHICKEN MARSALA

SERVINGS: 2 PREP TIME: 15 min. COOK TIME: 30 min.

CARBS – 15 g   FAT – 8 g   PROTEIN – 4 g   CALORIES – 140

INGREDIENTS

1 pounds boneless skinless chicken breasts, pounded ¼" thick
½ Tbsp all-purpose flour
salt and black pepper, to taste
1 Tbsp olive oil
½ Tbsp unsalted butter, divided
4 oz button mushrooms, sliced
1½ Tbsp shallots, finely chopped
2 cloves garlic, minced
½ cup chicken broth
½ cup dry Marsala wine
½ cup heavy cream
1 tsp chopped fresh thyme
1 Tbsp chopped fresh parsley, for serving

DIRECTIONS

Add flour, ¾ tsp salt, and ¼ tsp pepper in a Ziplock bag.
Place chicken in the bag and seal it. Shake to coat evenly. Set aside.

3. Over medium-high, heat oil and 2 Tbsps butter in a large skillet.
4. Place chicken in the pan, shaking off excess flour, and cook for 3-4 minutes per side until golden and barely cooked through. Transfer to a plate and set aside.
5. Melt 1 Tbsp butter in the pan.
6. Add mushrooms and cook for 3-4 minutes, occasionally stirring until they begin to brown.
7. Add shallots, garlic, and ¼ tsp of salt. Cook for 1-2 minutes more.
8. Add broth, heavy cream, Marsala, thyme, ¼ tsp salt, and ⅛ tsp pepper.
9. Let it boil, turn to medium, and cook for 10-15 minutes until it is reduced by half and slightly thickened.
10. Back chicken back to the pan, along with any juices that accumulated on the plate. Reduce to low and simmer for 2-3 minutes more. Sprinkle with parsley, if using.

GREEK CHICKEN PITAS WITH CUCUMBER & ORZO-FETA SALAD

SERVINGS: 2 PREP TIME: 10 min. COOK TIME: 30 min.

CARBS – 83 g FAT – 23 g PROTEIN – 51 g CALORIES – 750

INGREDIENTS

- *2 boneless, skinless chicken breasts*
- *3 oz orzo pasta*
- *2 pitas*
- *½ cup plain Greek yogurt*
- *2 cloves garlic, smashed*
- *1 cucumber, peeled and diced*
- *1 lemon, quartered*
- *1 bunch mint leaves*
- *1 bunch oregano, stems removed*
- *¼ cup crumbled feta cheese*
- *1 oz kalamata olives, smashed*

DIRECTIONS

1. Heat a pot filled with salted water to boiling on high.
2. Pat dry chicken with paper towels and season with salt and pepper.
3. In a pan, heat oil on medium-high.
4. Add chicken and cook for 4- 6 minutes per side, until cooked through. Remove to a cutting board.
5. To make dressing, mix oregano, half garlic paste, 2 lemon wedges juice, and drizzle with olive oil in a bowl. Season with salt and pepper.
6. When cool enough, slice cooked chicken. Add to the dressing bowl and toss to coat.
7. Mix yogurt, half cucumber, half mint, lemon juice, and garlic paste in a bowl. Add oil, salt and pepper. Stir to combine.
8. Heat the pan on medium-high.
9. Warm pitas – one at one time – for 1 minute per side. Transfer to a cutting board and cut in half.
10. Add, olives, remaining cucumber, cheese, remaining mint to the pot of cooked pasta, and drizzle with oil. Stir to combine.
11. Transfer to a serving plate and fill halved pitas with cucumber chicken.

GREEK CHICKEN GYROS

SERVINGS: 2 PREP TIME: 15 min. COOK TIME: 1 h.

CARBS – 15 g FAT – 8 g PROTEIN – 4 g CALORIES – 140

INGREDIENTS

½ pounds boneless chicken thighs
½ red onion
2 pitas
½ cup Tatziki sauce

FOR GYRO MARINADE

¾ Tbsp finely chopped garlic.
¾ Tbsp lemon juice
½ tsp whole pepper corns
⅓ cup extra-virgin olive oil
¾ Tbsp paprika powder
1 Tbsp dried rosemary
1 Tbsp whole coriander seeds
1 Tbsp dried red chili flakes
coarse sea salt to taste

DIRECTIONS

Preheat oven at 375°F.
Pound each chicken thigh until ½" thick
with a meat mallet. Set aside.

3. Add paprika, coriander, peppercorns, rosemary, chili flakes, and salt in a mortar and pestle to a semi-coarse powder.
4. Add chopped garlic and grind it until garlic blends with the rest of spice blend.
5. Pour in oil and lemon juice and mix well.
6. Add marinade to chicken thighs and mix until all the chicken thighs are evenly coated.
7. Wrap container, using a cling film, and leave overnight in the fridge to marinate.
8. Take a large onion stump and stick a bamboo skewer in the center of stump to create a vertical pole.
9. Put each chicken thigh and skewer them individually in the home-made vertical rotisserie.
10. Bake for 1 hour by placing vertical rotisserie over a cookie tray.
11. Let it cool for 15 minutes. Shave chicken meat and serve with Tzatziki sauce.

GREEK CHICKEN IN TOMATO-KOTOPOULO KOKKINISTO

SERVINGS: 2 PREP TIME: 10 min. COOK TIME: 1 h.

CARBS – 3 g FAT – 16 g PROTEIN – 19 g CALORIES – 226

INGREDIENTS

- *½ pound chicken in pieces*
- *½ onion, diced*
- *1 Tbsp olive oil*
- *1 minced garlic clove*
- *¼ cup water*
- *5 ounces diced tomatoes*
- *1 cinnamon stick*
- *1-2 allspice berries*
- *1 bay leaf*
- *salt and pepper, to taste*

DIRECTIONS

1. Heat olive oil and cook chicken pieces on both sides for 4-5 minutes in a large deep pan.
2. Set chicken aside and add onion. Cook until soft. Add garlic and cook for 1 minute.
3. Add ⅓ cup water, tomato, cinnamon stick, bay leaf, allspice, salt, and pepper and mix well. Add chicken and blend.
4. Cover and simmer until cooked, for 45 minutes.
5. Serve warm with preferable side-dish.

GREEK CHICKEN AND POTATOES

SERVINGS: 2 PREP TIME: 30 min. COOK TIME: 1 h.

CARBS – 41 g FAT – 12 g PROTEIN – 44 g CALORIES – 468

INGREDIENTS

1 whole chicken
2 lemons juice
⅓ cup extra-virgin olive oil
2 Tbsp dried oregano
11 cloves garlic, minced
4 medium potatoes, quartered
salt and pepper, to taste

DIRECTIONS

Preheat oven to 350°F. Cover a sheet pan with parchment paper.

Place chicken on a cutting board breast-side-down. Using a knife, cut chicken in half along the back bone. Turn it over and cut through the center of breast bone. Divide two halves and lay them on prepared pan skin-side-up.

3. Squeeze 1 lemon juice onto chicken, and rub it into whole chicken. Coat with olive oil and rub again to coat the skin. Season chicken with salt and pepper. Sprinkle 1 Tbsp oregano and half garlic over chicken.

4. Put potatoes in a large bowl. Add the rest olive oil, garlic, oregano, and 1 lemon juice, salt, and pepper. Toss to coat.

5. Arrange potatoes on the sheet pan around the chicken.

6. Roast for 1 hour 15 minutes until chicken is cooked through, and both are golden and crispy.

MEDITERRANEAN SAUTEED CHICKEN

SERVINGS: 2 PREP TIME: 10 min. COOK TIME: 20 min.

CARBS – 7 g FAT – 6 g PROTEIN – 29 g CALORIES – 222

INGREDIENTS

- *1 tsp olive oil*
- *1 Tbsp white wine*
- *2 skinless, boneless chicken breast halves*
- *2 cloves garlic, minced*
- *¼ cup diced onion*
- *2 cups cherry tomatoes*
- *¼ cup white wine*
- *1 tsp chopped fresh thyme*
- *3 tsp fresh basil*
- *¼ cup kalamata olives*
- *⅛ cup chopped fresh parsley*
- *Salt and pepper, to taste*

DIRECTIONS

1. Heat 2 Tbsps white wine and the oil in a large skillet over medium-low heat.
2. Add chicken and saute about 4-6 minutes each side, until golden-brown. Remove chicken from the skillet. Set aside.
3. Saute garlic in pan for 30 seconds, then add onion and saute for 3 minutes.
4. Add cherry tomatoes and bring to a boil.
5. Lower the heat and add the rest white wine. Simmer approximately 10 minutes.
6. Add basil and thyme and simmer for 5 minutes.
7. Put the chicken back in the skillet and cover.
8. Cook over the low heat until the chicken is cooked and no longer pink inside.
9. Add parsley and olives to the skillet and cook for 1 minute.
10. Season with pepper and salt to taste.

CHICKEN STUFFED WITH CHEESE

SERVINGS: 2 PREP TIME: 10 min. COOK TIME: 20 min.

CARBS – 3 g FAT – 22 g PROTEIN – 33 g CALORIES – 339

INGREDIENTS

2 chicken boneless, skinless breasts, pounded thin
¼ cup feta cheese
2 ounces cream cheese, softened
½ tsp garlic powder
1 Tbsp melted butter
1 tsp dried dill weed
Salt and pepper, to taste

DIRECTIONS

1. Preheat oven to 350°F.
2. Beat the cream cheese in a large bowl until smooth.
3. Add the feta cheese, garlic powder, and dill weed. Beat until creamy, smooth texture.
4. On each breast put ½ of the filling, then roll and tie the breasts with the cooking string to seal.
5. Brush every breast with melted butter and sprinkle with pepper and salt.
6. Bake uncovered for 20 minutes or until the juices run clear.

GREEK LEMONY CHICKEN SKEWERS

SERVINGS: 4 PREP TIME: 20 min. COOK TIME: 10 min. + 30 min. to marinate chicken

CARBS – 2 g FAT – 2 g PROTEIN – 32 g CALORIES – 166

INGREDIENTS

- *1 pound boneless, skinless chicken breasts*
- *1 Tbsp dried oregano leaves*
- *2 large cloves garlic, minced*
- *½ tsp grated lemon rind*
- *3 Tbsps lemon juice*
- *Pinch freshly ground pepper*

FOR TZATZIKI SAUCE:

- *⅔ cup 0% Greek yogurt*
- *⅓ cup shredded cucumber, squeezed dry*
- *1 small clove garlic, minced*
- *1 Tbsp fresh dill, chopped*
- *½ tsp lemon zest*

DIRECTIONS

1. Cut chicken breasts into 1" strips and chop every strip into 1½" chunks.

2. Place in a bowl and add garlic, oregano, pepper, lemon rind, and juice. Stir to coat well. Cover and refrigerate about 30 minutes.

3. In a separate bowl, stir yogurt, cucumber, dill, garlic, and lemon zest until combined. Cover and refrigerate 24 hours.

4. Preheat broiler to high, or if using the grill, preheat to medium-high.

5. Skewer chicken onto 4 metal or soaked wooden skewers.

6. If using a broiler, place skewers on a foil-lined baking sheet and place sheet in the oven, about 6 inches from broiler. Turn once after 8 minutes or until golden-browned and no longer pink inside.

7. If using a grill, place chicken skewers on greased grill over medium heat for about 10 minutes. Turn once.

8. Garnish with tzatziki sauce.

PANNA COTTA

SERVINGS: 2 PREP TIME: 5 min. COOK TIME: 10 min. + 4 h.

CARBS – 6 g FAT – 9 g PROTEIN – 1 g CALORIES – 105

INGREDIENTS

⅓ cup skim milk
1 (0.25-ounce) envelope unflavored gelatin
2½ cups heavy cream
½ cup white sugar
1½ tsps vanilla extract
⅓ cup red berries for decoration

DIRECTIONS

Pour milk into a small bowl and stir in the envelope of gelatin. Set aside.
Add the heavy cream and sugar to a saucepan, stirring, and set over medium-low heat. Watching carefully, let it come to a full boil.

3. Pour the gelatin-milk mixture into the cream, stirring until completely dissolved. Cook for one minute, stirring.
4. Take away from heat, stir in the vanilla extract and pour into six ramekin dishes.
5. Allow to cool to room temperature.
6. Before serving, cover with plastic wrap and freeze for at least 4 hours, but preferably overnight. Top with red berries before serving.

TURKISH KUNEFE

SERVINGS: 2 PREP TIME: 10 min. COOK TIME: 55 min.

CARBS – 57 g FAT – 25 g PROTEIN – 19 g CALORIES – 508

INGREDIENTS

FOR SYRUP:
- 1 cup sugar
- 1 slice of lemon
- 1 cup water

FOR KUNEFE:
- ½ cup butter melted to room temperature
- 1 Tbsp butter for pans
- 2 cups shredded raw kadayif dough
- ½ cup unsalted melting cheese of your choice
- 1 Tbsp ground pistachios

DIRECTIONS

1. In a pot, add all syrup ingredients.
2. Bring to a boil, then reduce heat to medium-low and simmer for 15 minutes until it gets a little thicker. Allow to cool.
3. Preheat the stove to 400° F.
4. Put kadayif dough to a bowl and coat with ½ cup melted butter.
5. Lightly brush the bottom of four 9" pans with melted butter.
6. Devide the half of the dough in two pans evenly. Press it with your hand.
7. Sprinkle noodles with cheese evenly. Press with your hand.
8. Cover with the remaining kadayif dough and press it with your hand.
9. Put to oven and bake for 10-15 minutes or until the top is golden-brown.
10. Turn each of two extra pans over, carefully place it above the dessert and flip the dessert into that extra pan. Now golden-brown side is on the bottom. Put it back to oven and bake for 10-15 minutes more or until the top side is golden-brown as well.
11. As soon as you remove dessert from the stove, pour syrup over them.
12. Allow syrup to absorb and serve immediately while it's still hot, topping wit ground pistachios.

CREMA CATALANA

SERVINGS: 2 PREP TIME: 3 h. COOK TIME: 10 min.

CARBS – 61 g FAT – 10 g PROTEIN – 12 g CALORIES – 372

INGREDIENTS

4 large egg yolks
1 cup sugar
1 cinnamon stick
Zest of 1 lemon
2 cups whole milk
1 Tbsp cornstarch

DIRECTIONS

1. Whisk ¾ cup sugar and the egg yolks in a large saucepan until the ingredients are thoroughly mixed and the mixture becomes frothy.
2. Add the lemon zest and cinnamon stick.
3. Add the cornstarch and milk and heat the mixture slowly, stirring constantly, just until it begins to thicken. Remove the pot from the heat immediately.
4. Remove the cinnamon stick and pour the mixture into 2 ramekins to cool.
5. Cool to room temperature, then freeze for at least 2-3 hours.
6. Before serving, heat the broiler. Sprinkle the sugar over each ramekin. Place the ramekins under the broiler and let the sugar caramelize, bubble, and turn golden brown, about 5-10 minutes. Remove and serve immediately.

SPANISH DESSERT TURRON

SERVINGS: 2 bites PREP TIME: 15 min. COOK TIME: 15 min.

CARBS – 16 g FAT – 14 g PROTEIN – 6 g CALORIES – 216

INGREDIENTS

- *1 cup baked almond*
- *100 g honey*
- *100 g sugar*
- *2 pieces egg white*
- *1 piece waffles*
- *1 cup hazelnut*

DIRECTIONS

1. Add nuts in a blender and chop for 10-15 seconds. Keep large pieces.
2. Cover baking form using a waffle paper.
3. Combine sugar and honey in a saucepan and melt on low heat.
4. Whisk egg whites. Combine nuts with egg whites and stir gently. Add nut paste to honey mix and cook for 10 minutes more on very low heat. It should have a light caramel color.
5. Spread it evenly onto the baking form. Let it chill in a cold place, and NOT IN THE FRIDGE.

PALAČINKE – SERBIAN PANCAKE

SERVINGS: 2 PREP TIME: 5 min. COOK TIME: 15 min.

CARBS – 15 g FAT – 8 g PROTEIN – 4 g CALORIES – 140

INGREDIENTS

1 cup flour
2 eggs
½ cup milk
½ cup water
¼ tsp salt
2 Tbsp butter, melted

DIRECTIONS

1. Mix all components until you get a homogeneous batter. Break apart any granules.
2. Grease a crepe pan with oil or melted butter. Wait till it's hot.
3. Pour enough batter to coat the whole pan with one thin layer, swirling your wrist while you holding the pan.
4. If you lift a corner of crepe off the pan, using a knife, and it doesn't stick, then it's ready to be flipped over. If not, give it a few more seconds. Transfer to the plate when it's golden.
5. Repeat for the rest batter. Makes two portions of five thin pancakes.

ALMOND TANGERINE PANNA COTTA

SERVINGS: 2 PREP TIME: 15 min. COOK TIME: 1 h. 15 min.

CARBS – 16 g FAT – 13 g PROTEIN – 3 g CALORIES – 193

INGREDIENTS

- 1½ Tbsp sugar
- ¾ tsp unflavored gelatin
- ½ cup fat-free milk
- ½ cup plain Greek yogurt
- ¼ tsp almond extract

FOR SAUCE
- 1 Tbsp sugar
- 1 tsp cornstarch
- ⅓ cup pomegranate or cranberry juice
- ½ cup tangerine sections
- 2 Tbsp snipped dried tart cherries

DIRECTIONS

1. Place 4 6 oz ramekins in a baking pan.
2. Mix gelatin and sugar in a saucepan.
3. Add in milk, and dissolve gelatin heating it and stirring over medium heat.
4. Remove from heat, add in yogurt and ¼ almond extract and whisk until smooth.
5. Pour mixture in ramekins, cover, and chill for 4-24 hours to let it set.
6. To make sauce, mix cornstarch and sugar in a small saucepan. Add in pomegranate juice, and cook until thickened and bubbling over medium heat, stirring all the time.
7. Remove from heat, and add in tangerine, cherries, and ¼ tsp almond extract. Let it cool.
8. When ready to serve, immerse bottom half of ramekins for 10 seconds in hot water. Using a sharp knife, loosen panna cotta from the ramekin's sides.
9. Invert a plate over each cup and turn it together.
10. Remove cups and serve panna cotta with sauce.

ZABAGLIONE WITH STRAWBERRIES

SERVINGS: 2 PREP TIME: 5 min. COOK TIME: 10 min.

CARBS – 30 g FAT – 11 g PROTEIN – 7 g CALORIES – 205

INGREDIENTS

4 egg yolks, at room temperature
½ cup dry marsala
¼ cup sugar
½ pint strawberries, sliced

DIRECTIONS

1. Add egg yolks, marsala, and sugar into a double boiler.
2. Beat mixture for 4-7 minutes with hand mixer on low until it is hot and forms a ribbon when the beaters are lifted. DO NOT cook mixture for too long, or it will start to curdle.
3. Put strawberries in the glasses. Top with the hot zabaglione and serve or refrigerate it for 1 hour.

MUHALABIEH

SERVINGS: 2   PREP TIME: 10 min.   COOK TIME: 10 min.

CARBS – 36 g   FAT – 3 g   PROTEIN – 4 g   CALORIES – 162

INGREDIENTS

- *½ cup (250 ml) milk*
- *⅛ cup (50 grams) sugar*
- *¾ Tbsp cornflour*
- *¼ Tbsp rose water*
- *pistachios for garnish*

DIRECTIONS

1. Heat milk over medium in a saucepan.
2. Add sugar, cornflour, and rose water.
3. Whisk until milk starts to get thicker.
4. When it starts to get a cream-like consistency, remove from heat.
5. Prepare 4 glass bowls, and divide the mixture between them.
6. Let it cool down, then place in the fridge and chill for 2 hours.
7. When completely chilled, flip over on a serving plate and garnish with chopped pistachios.

Thank you for reading this book and having the patience to try the recipes.

I do hope that you have had as much enjoyment reading and experimenting with the meals as I have had writing the book.

Stay safe and healthy!

RECIPE INDEX

Dry Weights

OZ	🥄	C	⚖️	⚖️
1/2 OZ	1 Tbsp	1/16 C	15 g	
1 OZ	2 Tbsp	1/8 C	28 g	
2 OZ	4 Tbsp	1/4 C	57 g	
3 OZ	6 Tbsp	1/3 C	85 g	
4 OZ	8 Tbsp	1/2 C	115 g	1/4 lb
8 OZ	16 Tbsp	1 C	227 g	1/2 lb
12 OZ	24 Tbsp	1 1/2 C	340 g	3/4 lb
16 OZ	32 Tbsp	2 C	455 g	1 lb

Liquid Conversions

1 Gallon:
4 quarts
8 pints
16 cups
128 fl oz
3.8 liters

1 Quart:
2 pints
4 cups
32 fl oz
0.95 liters

1 Pint:
2 cups
16 fl oz
480 ml

1 Cup:
16 Tbsp
8 fl oz
240 ml

OZ	🥄	🥄	mL	C	Pt	Qt
1 oz	6 tsp	2 Tbsp	30 ml	1/8 C		
2 oz	12 tsp	4 Tbsp	60 ml	1/4 C		
2 2/3 oz	16 tsp	5 Tbsp	80 ml	1/3 C		
4 oz	24 tsp	8 Tbsp	120 ml	1/2 C		
5 1/3 oz	32 tsp	11 Tbsp	160 ml	2/3 C		
6 oz	36 tsp	12 Tbsp	177 ml	3/4 C		
8 oz	48 tsp	16 Tbsp	237 ml	1 C	1/2 pt	1/4 qt
16 oz	96 tsp	32 Tbsp	480 ml	2 C	1 pt	1/2 qt
32 oz	192 tsp	64 Tbsp	950 ml	4 C	2 pt	1 qt

Fahrenheit to Celcius (F to C)

500 F = 260 C
475 F = 245 C
450 F = 235 C
425 F = 220 C
400 F = 205 C
375 F = 190 C
350 F = 180 C
325 F = 160 C
300 F = 150 C
275 F = 135 C
250 F = 120 C
225 F = 107 C

1 Tbsp: 15 ml

1 tsp: 5 ml

Safe Cooking Meat Temperatures

Minimum temperatures:

USDA Safe at 145 F — USDA Safe at 160 F — USDA Safe at 165 F

Beef Steaks, Briskets, and Roasts; Pork Chops, Roasts, Ribs, Shoulders, and Butts; Lamb Chops, Legs, and Roasts; Fresh Hams, Veal Steaks, Fish, and Shrimp

Ground Meats (except poultry)

Chicken & Turkey, ground or whole

Printed in the USA
CPSIA information can be obtained
at www.ICGtesting.com
CBHW050709100624
9801CB00026B/125